W9-ASK-167

F

That the World May Believe

That the World May Believe

by HANS KÜNG

translated by Cecily Hastings

SHEED AND WARD—*New York*

Not for them only do I pray, but for them also who through their word shall believe in me: that they all may be one, as thou, Father, in me, and I in thee: that they also may be one in us; THAT THE WORLD MAY BELIEVE. . . .

John xvii. 20-21

Contents

Instead of a Preface

SOME PEOPLE may find it odd that I should have written to you so often. A University professor is generally supposed to have more high-powered things to do in the way of lectures, seminars, research, etc. As it happens, I kept up with all that quite happily, including the writing of a large tome with a load of footnotes: tough theological fare, not for you. But this is your book. These are private letters, written not for theologians but for you. Doing theology, which is at this present time faced with a number of unresolved and extremely difficult problems in the teaching of the Church, would involve going further and deeper into things than this. Here, I am not trying to develop and solve those problems, but to give simple answers to your questions. I wrote these letters for you because I know the things that trouble you. You don't find things easy, although you don't show it and don't care much for talking about "the faith." That was why you wrote to me. And to be quite frank, you know, and just between ourselves, these letters that you asked me for were no trouble to me. I really liked writing them to you, even quite late at night. I knew how you looked forward to getting my answers, so I tried not to delay any longer than necessary. It's after midnight now, as a matter of fact; being a professor isn't always the easiest thing in the world! So God bless you for now. When shall I be hearing from you again?

Tübingen, May 1962

That the World May Believe

FIRST LETTER

Do you discuss things with Protestants?

I AM GLAD you have come up against this. It really is a problem, and not an easy one. I can well believe that you are puzzling over it and don't quite know how to deal with it. It certainly is a good thing that you and Yvonne should have begun to talk about your religion. Before, you used just to take it for granted, didn't you? You were Catholic, Yvonne Protestant: that was how it was. So were her parents and grandparents Protestants, for the matter of that, just as yours were Catholics. But you are right, both of you: it isn't really all that normal. On the contrary, it's downright abnormal. Because, as you very well know, Christ certainly did not found two Churches, but *one*; and in the last hours before he suffered, he prayed that we who believe in him should all be *one*. He even said that we should be one as he and the Father are one.

It is in fact a tragedy—and you two sensed this a little in your discussion—that Christendom should

15

have fallen apart into so many groups. As you say, you and Yvonne are so thoroughly in sympathy with each other about everything: there is nothing you can't talk about, nothing you can't make contact over; just this one one thing, and it alone, when you go into the presence of God, you cannot go together. You have to separate, and go, you into a Catholic, Yvonne into a Protestant church. Once there, you each pray your own special prayers and sing your own special hymns and do your own special religious service. Your churches are quite close to each other, you can hear each other's bells, and you seem to be so far apart in your faith. And all the time—how right you are—this is just where unity is most important. You can have different opinions about a book or a film, but in your faith there ought to be just *one* conviction.

Isn't it necessary, you ask, to hurry up and arrive at union? Yes, it certainly is. But you must also realize that the great mountainous barrier that has been thrown up between Catholics and Protestants cannot be removed overnight. When you have a deep schism that has lasted four hundred years it is not possible to bring it to an end from one day to the next simply by declaring it over. It calls for endless goodwill, endless work, thought, study and discussion, and above all endless prayer; you can do your share, it depends on you too. If we Catholics and Protestants are ever to come together again, we cannot do it by our own powers; God himself will have to grant it to us. The fact that since that discussion you have been praying for Yvonne in a quite new way is a good thing. But it is just as important that you should pray (as I am sure you will) for the removal of this detestable, disastrous schism; that you should pray for the unity of Christians. No one is going to achieve the unity of Christians as from tomorrow: the reunion of Catholics with Lutherans, with the Orthodox of the East, with Anglicans and American Episcopalians, etc. But we can *prepare* for it: we can take steps, large, bold steps, towards reunion. The Catholic Church longs to take the lead in doing everything that she can for reunion. This is a great and difficult task.

You ask, too, how you ought to handle a discussion of that sort with Yvonne. I realize that you often don't know what to answer. Are there any rules about this? Not really. You always have to see afresh what's best in this particular case. It always depends on whom you are talking to, and what about. But I can give you a few suggestions which strike me as important; they won't tell you what answers to give in detail, but just what general attitude to take up, what basic approach to have in a discussion of this sort.

First of all: *never forget that Protestants are Christians too!* You realized yourself that Yvonne believes as you do in God the Father, who created heaven and earth. Yvonne believes as you do in Jesus Christ, the Father's Son, our Lord, who was conceived by the Holy Ghost, born of the Virgin Mary, suffered under Pontius Pilate, was crucified, died and was buried, but who rose again the third day from the dead and now sits at the right hand of the Father until he comes again to judge the living and the dead. And Yvonne believes as you do in the Holy Ghost, the holy, catholic (that is, universal) Church, the communion of saints, the forgiveness of sins, the resurrection of the body and everlasting life. And furthermore, as you know, Yvonne believes as you do in everything that is written in Holy Scripture; indeed, she told you that in her family the Scripture is read more often than I am afraid it is in yours. And what is particularly important is that Yvonne is baptized, as you are, in the name of the Father and the Son and the Holy Ghost. Towards the end of your letter you ask whether her baptism was real baptism. Certainly, it was real, valid baptism, just as much as your own, so that she would

not have to be baptized again even if she were to become a Catholic, which, as you say, she does not want
in the least. You see, in a certain sense we can say that
it was chance that made you a Catholic and Yvonne
a Protestant; it was in the one Christian baptism that
you were both baptized. If you had been brought up
in Yvonne's parents' house, the overwhelming probability is that you would have been a Protestant, and
the same applies to her the other way round. So, since
Yvonne cannot help having been born and brought
up a Protestant, it cannot be regarded as her fault.
Not that it is unimportant what Church you spend
your life in; I'll be making that clearer shortly. But
the other side of it is true as well: Yvonne can be in
God's grace and can win eternal life if she lives according to her conscience and keeps God's commandments. This is a comfort, isn't it? You may be
separated on the way, but not in the eternal goal. And
even as concerns the way in this world, what unites
Catholics and Protestants as Christians is incompa-
rably more vast than what—alas, all too clearly—
separates them.

Secondly: *Remember that not only Protestants
but we Catholics are responsible for the schism!* You
and I, living today, cannot of course simply abolish

the schism; nor did we cause it. We inherited it, like a family debt, a family burden, weighing more heavily on us today than it ever has before. A debt which our ancestors (and Yvonne's) contracted four hundred years ago. People at that time wanted to improve the Church, to reform her; all the good people in the Church wanted it, it was a task that had become pressingly overdue. But we Catholics cannot regard it as justified that, for the sake of this reform of the Church, the Protestants separated themselves, four hundred years ago, from the successors of the apostles, and especially from the successor of St. Peter, and left our Church. Nor can we see it as justified today. But we should have to be complete Pharisees to look for all the faults on the other side. A real Christian looks for faults in himself first, so as not to see the mote in someone else's eye while ignoring the beam in his own. The Protestants didn't separate themselves from us over nothing. You must have learned at school, in religion classes and history classes, that four hundred years ago there was a great deal in our Church which was badly wrong and which it seemed hardly possible to put right: things involving the Pope, the bishops, the priests and the Catholic people. It was because our Catholic Church was in a bad state and people despaired of its ever getting better that the Protestants left it. If our Church had been in a better state, the Protestants would not have separated themselves from us. You see how wrong it would be if we Catholics prided ourselves on being absolutely and entirely in the right. We must, on the contrary, discuss things very humbly with Protestants. Yvonne will feel at once whether you are discussing her beliefs arrogantly or humbly.

The second point leads to the third: *Always remember that we Catholics have things to put right as well.* Protestant Christians have some quite definite demands which they make of us, and to a great extent they are justified demands. They had them four hundred years ago; we have fulfilled quite a number of them in the meanwhile, many things in the Church have been improved. But we have not done anything like everything that Protestants expect of us, things we really could do very much better if we really wanted to live according to the Gospel. There is still a lot to be done. You can quite well ask Yvonne yourself about things that she would like to see changed in us.

Which brings me to my last piece of advice: *try to get to know both the Protestant faith and your own*

Catholic faith better. One doesn't always reach immediate understanding over matters of faith. Explanations aren't always so easy. But just ask, and try to understand. You can get a lot of light that way: a lot that will be useful to you, yourself. On many questions you are sure to find that you are not well enough prepared to answer, or at least to answer well. This does not matter. It will make you realize, as it is time that you should, that you cannot grow physically and mentally without growing in the faith as well. You can't walk far in baby shoes, meaning by catechism. So do your best to get to know your faith better, and to deepen it: by prayer and Scripture reading, by good books, and by discussion with your chaplain and in your group. That way, you will be able to shed a little light on things for Yvonne, too. And you will both be surprised to find, in so many things, how close you are to each other in your faith.

If you come and see me again sometime, we shall be able to discuss plenty of things better in conversation. Give my love to Yvonne. All the best to yourself.

Let us pray to the Holy Ghost for Catholic and Protestant Christians:

that they take their stand not on schools of thought but on the Gospel of Christ,

that they may have no desire to "win" in discussion,

that truth and love be wholly identified in them,

that they should strive not to perpetuate differences but to resolve them,

that their hearts' desire should be not the drawing of frontiers but the finding of common ground.

Does a Catholic have to defend everything?

So THEY were attacking you. Not viciously, you say, but violently. It wasn't against you, but against your Church—our Church. The Church's teaching—the dogma of the Assumption, the dogma of the Immaculate Conception, papal infallibility. The Church's practice—the superstition and miracle-fever and apparition-mania in so many of the faithful, devotion to our Lady swamping the thought of Christ, Vatican politics, persecution of Protestants in Spain and South America, out-of-date pomp surrounding the Pope and bishops in their etiquette and titles and dress, a Latin liturgy that no one can understand, the Index. . . . Yes, you had rather a lot to listen to all at once, and you felt a bit discouraged after trying that discussion. You were several times driven into a corner, and it was hard to find an answer. It was possible to counter-attack, and that was often your best defense. But it was a defense that didn't satisfy you. It is unsatisfactory to make a sortie through one gate when it means that you are leaving another, open and undefended, behind you. What's to be done? you ask.

You were right to defend the Church. For a Catholic, it goes without saying that he must have the courage to bear witness, to bear witness to Christ and hence to the Church. And you were able, in fact, to explain a great deal, to clear up a great many misunderstandings. It was lucky that you had gone a bit further than your catechism. Everything that you've learned about the Church in your group, everything that you've read in books and periodicals, everything that you've got from discussions with your chaplain, all came to your help. But you felt the gaps, too. And what worried you more was that you felt some doubts. Quite serious doubts about whether there really is an answer at all to some things, whether a lot of the things of which the Church is accused don't simply have to be admitted, whether we like it or not.

Well, does a Catholic really have to *defend every-thing*? Our Church doesn't expect you to call black white. She doesn't expect you to paint her situation in rosy colors. She doesn't expect lies, or whitewash, or evasion. All she expects from you is *the truth*, neither more nor less. Our Church is very well aware that she is a Church of *human beings*. The Pope is a human being, the bishops are human beings, the parish priests and curates are human beings, all the faithful, you and I included, are human beings. And where you have human beings, you have things that are human, and all *too* human: you get staleness and failure, mediocrity, deviations, deformations, impoverishment, fossilization and narrowness, wrong decisions and wrong developments. It's not for nothing that even the infallibility of the Pope is limited to those few, exceptional cases in which the Pope as supreme teacher and shepherd of the Church makes a definitive, binding statement of the faith for the whole Church. Since the definition of infallibility at the first Vatican Council nearly a hundred years ago, this has happened only once, in the dogma of our Lady's Assumption, proclaimed in 1950. In everything else that he says and does, according to the common teaching of the Church, the Pope *can* be radically mistaken, though of course he does not *have* to be mistaken. And what is possible for the Pope is certainly possible at the lower levels of the Church's hierarchy—the bishops, parish priests and curates. A Catholic can sometimes try to *explain* some of the all too human wrong decisions and wrong developments which have thus occurred, and do occur, in the course of centuries in this human Church, but he does not need to *defend* it all. The fact that Rome forbade the famous astronomer Galileo, and with him all other Catholics, to hold that the earth goes round the sun, as being contrary to Scripture, was a wrong decision, and a decision with very grave consequences for the attitude of the Church towards modern science. The fact that all translations of the Canon of the Mass into the vernacular (i.e. all missals for popular use) were on the Index of forbidden books until 1897 is not something which we of today are going to regard as a sound development. There is a great deal of pomp in the matter of clothes and titles in our Church which is no longer going to be seen today either as appropriate to our times or as harmonizing with the simplicity of Christ and his apostles; and so on, and so on. In the eyes of those outside her, the Church is smothered by all these things; to a great extent, they make her incredible to them. All this is not a help "that the world may believe," but a hindrance. A loyal Catholic does not have to defend all this, or much else besides; he never has to speak against the truth. All this belongs to the human side of the Church, even to her all too human side. The Church is not indeed *of* this world, but she is *in* this visible, human world, and the visible, human world is in the Church.

But besides this, there are not only wrong decisions and wrong developments in our Church, involving no one personally; there is also personal guilt, sin, in our Church. She is not only a Church of human beings but a Church of *sinners*. None of us can count ourselves out: "In many things we all offend," says St. James (iii. 2). Or, as St. John says in his first Epistle: "If we say that we have no sin, we deceive ourselves and the truth is not in us" (i. 8). It is not for nothing that we all say the Confiteor at every Mass: "I confess to almighty God that I have sinned exceedingly in thought, word and deed, through my fault, through my fault, through my most grievous fault." *Everyone* says the Confiteor: Pope, bishops, priests, you and I and all the faithful. In all the members of the Church, high and low, there is sin and vice. There have been bad laymen, bad priests and bishops, bad Popes, and there always will be. So a Catholic does not need to defend and whitewash the bad Popes of the tenth century and the Renaissance, nor to defend and play down the bad state that the clergy and people were in at the time of the Reformation. This is all part of the sinfulness of the Church. It is true that the

Church is not of this world, but she is in this sinful world, and the sinful world is in the Church.

This is the situation, you see. You don't need to defend everything. In fact, it wouldn't be a good thing, for you or for the Church, if you did defend everything. The whole point, as the Gospel tells us, is "*that the world may believe*." You, as a witness to the truth, would be making our Church into something that could not be believed in, if you made error into truth and sin into virtue. What happens when you defend the indefensible? The person you are discussing it with, whether unbeliever or separated believer, is then going to concentrate on the dark, shadow side of our Church, which you are trying to deny or minimize. He will try, and keep trying harder and harder, to convince you that there is this dark, shadow side to the Church; he will try to prove how vast and impenetrable it is; he will use all his knowledge to bring up more and more damaging material. In short, you will never come to any conclusion, and the discussion will be fruitless, both for you and for the Church.

But what happens if you *admit* what is indefensible? Then he will gradually come to see that you are not disputing that there is a dark, shadow side to the Church, but that this does not contradict your *faith* in the Church. Then, perhaps, with a little knowledge and skill, you will be able to get him to see, very slowly, that this shadow is not the only thing in the Church, that it isn't even the most important, characteristic thing in her, simply because a shadow never is the positive thing, but what is casting the shadow. And so perhaps, very slowly, you may manage to show that this darkness does not constitute the essence of the Church; that it is rather the all too human *anti-*essence of a Church consisting of human beings who are sinners; and that her real *essence* is the light: the light which she has received from God in our Lord Jesus Christ, and which she bears onwards "that the world may believe."

Do you see what I mean? Try having that discussion all over again!

That the Church may be glorious, without spot or wrinkle, is the final goal to which we are being led through the passion of Christ. It will be so only in our eternal home, not on our journey there, during which, if we said we had no sin, we should be deceiving ourselves, as we are told in the first Epistle of St. John.

—THOMAS AQUINAS.

If scandal is taken at the truth, then it is better to allow scandal to arise than to abandon the truth.

—POPE GREGORY THE GREAT.

THIRD LETTER

Is criticism enough?

THE GREAT PROTESTANT theologian Karl Barth said to me once, some time ago: "You Catholics are strange people! If any of you ever does manage to see that there's anything awry in your Church, or downright rotten, and even if he goes so far as to admit that it's so, then—well, what does he do then? He takes a deep breath, swallows the nasty mouthful down, digests it in a trice, and says, 'But I'm still a Catholic all the same!' And nothing else happens at all."

What do you think? You have heard the same sort of thing said: the Catholic Church, by contrast with the Protestant, is regarded as the non-reformed, the non-renewed Church. She is regarded as a Church which will, at best, admit criticism (and that not as often as she should), but which remains radically incorrigible. The old Church, where everything always carries on as of old! And this makes this Catholic Church of ours something that *cannot be believed*. It makes people unable to believe that *this* could be the true Church of Jesus Christ. She may be old and great and powerful, but she has to a great extent forgotten the Lord's Gospel, and she is more ready to adapt herself to the world than to re-adapt herself afresh to the Gospel. What, you ask, is one to say about this?

Now, does being a Catholic, when faced with the evil in the Church, really consist in swallowing it down? It certainly does *include* swallowing it down. This swallowing is something that all Christians have to do: to put up with the bad, shoddy, inadequate things in their Church, tolerate them and often keep quiet about them. Protestant Christians have to do it too, often no less than Catholics, in fact. The Church really does consist of human beings. And wherever there are human beings there is the all too human element: the element of viciousness, hatefulness, inadequacy, ill-will. Even in the Church, you can't make angels out of human beings. They go on being human, and everything that they touch, everything that they put into operation, is always a human work, pitifully fragile and imperfect. So there's nothing for it but to keep on putting up with a great deal in the persons and institutions in the Church, just as, after all, the other people in the Church have to put up with me in all my wretched humanity, and swallow down a great deal that I inflict on them.

All the same, as I wrote in my last letter, we can criticize. Often we not only can but must, at the right place and time. But is criticism enough? That is what you ask, and you yourself suggest the answer: it cannot be enough just to critize. What do you do when things get shabby around the house; when screws have worked loose in door or window frames, window panes have been broken (from inside or out!), and plaster and paint are peeling off the walls? Is it enough to stand there and produce intelligent (or unintelligent) criticism? No, you say, you have to get busy. Maybe you have to clear out a certain amount of dust and rubbish and do a really thorough cleaning; you have to knock in a few new nails, repair this and reinforce that, do some replacements and renewals. You are always having to renew a house, and the older it is the more it needs to be done.

You see what I mean. The Church too, as a building which men have built, is always having to be renewed, renovated, reformed. Of course the Church belongs, as his own property, to the Master-Builder, the Lord of Lords, and always will; but men have been allowed, as his servants, to join in the building of it. And, being men, they have done it as well and as badly as men do things. But it is our Lord's will that they should keep on taking trouble over it, keep on working at it afresh, doing everything according to his plan and pleasure. This is not a grim imposition but a delightful privilege. For he himself gives the strength for it, the strength which we of ourselves do not have. He gives us his Holy Spirit. It is the Spirit for whom we pray, and who constantly renews the face of the Church. But, by God's undeserved merciful goodness, we are allowed to be "God's co-adjutors," forever reconstructing the Church.

It is not true that the Catholic Church, by contrast with the Protestant, is an unreformed, unrenewed Church. You have perhaps read in a history of the Church, or at least you will have heard, how hard people worked—though, alas, not always hard enough —at renewing our Church, long before the Reformation. It was so already in the early Church. Again and again the Scriptures were translated out of their original languages into the languages of the people, and already established translations were reformed. Again and again preaching and instruction and theology were adapted to new nations and given new forms.

Again and again the liturgy of the Mass was altered and renewed. To take just one example, Mass was at first celebrated at Rome in Greek, because at that time people spoke Greek in Rome. Two hundred years later people were once more talking Latin at Rome, so the language of the whole Mass was changed and Latin introduced instead of Greek. Similarly, it is possible that soon Italian will be introduced in Rome and Italy instead of Latin, so that the people, who no longer speak Latin but Italian, will be able once more, as they were during the first thousand years, to understand all the readings, prayers and chants that go on at the altar, and to join in them in their mother tongue.

But it was not only in the early centuries but in the Middle Ages too that repeated efforts were made to renew the Church, which had now grown rich and worldly. The German Emperors started on it, and then the Popes as well. Most of all, the great saints who led or founded Orders worked for the reform of the Church: such as the most famous man of western Europe in the twelfth century, Bernard of Clairvaux, with the Cistercians, and then, in the thirteenth century, St. Dominic with the Dominicans, and above all the matchless St. Francis of Assisi with his Franciscans.

All the same, Church reform collapsed in the later Middle Ages, in spite of the efforts of several Councils. In many ways it was a very bad time in the Catholic Church. This led to Luther's great protest, and this in turn to his rebellion against the Catholic Church as she had existed until then, and to his expulsion from our Church. What Luther wanted was good in itself: he wanted the Church to frame herself and her theology anew according to the Gospel of Christ, to renew and reform herself. But there were other, less good, factors at work along with these good demands; and not least, politics. And so, for the sake of Church reform there came the tragedy of schism, which, as you know, has lasted until the present day. The Catholic Church could not accept Luther's way of Church reform for various reasons which I do not need to explain here; in that time of crisis Luther abandoned many things which must not be abandoned if one is really going to keep to the Scriptures.

So the Catholic Church rejected *Luther's* reform, but she did not by any means reject *all* Church reform. On the contrary, in the four hundred years since Luther the Catholic Church, aroused by Luther's thunderclap, has carried out a tremendous work of reform (though sometimes making rather heavy weather of it, moving slowly and inch by inch): reform of the papacy, the bishops, the priests, the people; reform of theology, liturgy, Church law, devotion. . . . In comparison with the very depressed Church of the Reformation period, the Catholic Church of today is to a great extent a renewed and reformed Church, so that it is not even quite certain whether Luther would have broken with the Catholic Church as she is today. And similarly, Protestants have in recent decades been carrying out a reform of many things. With Catholics and Protestants both renewing their Churches, with their eyes fixed on the same Gospel, they have drawn closer to each other to a considerable extent. All men of good will sincerely rejoice at this. But the Catholic Church is still in the middle of this process of renewal. There is an endless amount still to be done: renewal of the liturgy, of Scripture reading, of devotion, of theology, of pastoral and missionary work: all with a view to the reunion of separated Christians.

As you see, neither swallowing down nor criticizing is enough on its own. You have to have *action* as well: *that the world may believe!* We must clear out the things that our Lord does not want us to have in the Church. We must do the things that our Lord requires of the Church. There is no shortage of jobs. Are you going to help? Think out how you are going to do it!

CREDO ECCLESIAM SANCTAM

Catholic reform, being renewal, lies midway between two extremes, revolution and restoration.

Catholic reform is not revolution: it does not aim at the violent overthrow either of values or of authority; it is not bent upon what is new in a doctrinaire, fanatical fashion, without piety toward the past.

While fully aware of what is better in what is new, Catholic reform is intent upon preserving the continuity of historical development, and hence is not innovation but renewal.

Catholic reform is not restoration; it does not aim lethargically at the maintenance of a system but courageously advances toward ever greater truth. It has no wish to re-establish old forms, but to discover new forms appropriate to the times. It does not wish to tighten up the rigorous observance of laws, regula-

tions, canons and subsections and so revive some out-worn disciplinary system, but to renew the Church's institutions from within.

While fully aware of the value of ancient tradition, Catholic reform is intent upon that creative renewal of the Church's structure which the present demands. Hence it is not simply restoration but renewal. Catholic reform, being a renewal, is neither a purely interior reform of the heart nor a purely exterior reform of abuses, but a positive, creative reform of the state of the Church.

FOURTH LETTER

Was it always like this?

You were surprised by something I said, in passing, in my last letter, about the language of the Mass: wasn't it always as it is today? No, it wasn't. It was of course, all down the centuries, essentially the same Mass: the same thanksgiving ceremony, the same thanksgiving meal, in which we remember the great things that God has done for us in his Son Jesus Christ. You know how it is, that when some great thing has happened somewhere, people do not want it to be forgotten. So they put up a memorial tablet ("In this house lived and worked X, the famous. . . .") or memorial stone ("On this spot, in the year such-and-such. . . ."), or perhaps a magnificent monument ("In memory of the battle of. . . ."). It used also to be the custom to build memorial chapels or churches.

But these are all only dead memorials, lifeless signs. You also find living signs, memorial *ceremonies*. There are very impressive examples amongst many peoples.

The memorial ceremony includes a memorial *play,* as for example the William Tell play, which represents what Tell, according to the legend, did for his people. The events of many centuries ago are made once more into a living reality before the eyes of present-day spectators and participants. It becomes real to them all once more that the hero sacrificed himself then for the whole people. A memorial ceremony of this sort makes present again, in a very complete way, what happened then, many hundreds of years ago.

You already see what I mean: the Mass is a memorial ceremony of this kind, a ceremony of remembrance of everything that our Lord did for us. "Do this in memory of me, for a remembrance of me!" was what our Lord commanded. We did not invent this memorial ceremony for ourselves: we are simply carrying out the terms of our Lord's last will. This is why, in the middle of Mass, straight after Jesus' words "Do this in commemoration of me," we pray: "Therefore, Lord, *mindful* of the saving passion, resurrection from the dead and glorious ascension into heaven of your Son, our Lord Jesus Christ, we offer to your excellent Majesty, of your own gifts and presents, a pure victim. . . ." Thus what then happened becomes real for us again: not as a stage performance, but really and truly in our lives.

I am sure you understand now—it is absolutely essential to the Mass that it is a memorial ceremony. It is not simply something new that is being done. What is being celebrated here is something that in fact *happened*, though many centuries ago, at a particular place and a particular time. We are remembering a real historical event, which is still valid for us today and will never lose its value like, say, an old bank note. That is why the Scriptures are always read as part of the celebration of Mass: so that we shall remember the great saving acts of God in the Old and New Testaments; so that, above all, we shall remember the great battle of deliverance which Christ fought for the whole of mankind, to free us from sin and hence from suffering and death.

When a memorial ceremony is held today for some man who once sacrificed himself for his people at a time of sorrow and tragedy, this does not mean that the ceremony itself is something tragic. It was precisely his sacrificing himself that brought salvation and blessing to the people. Clearly, this applies to us too: when we celebrate the memory that the Son of God sacrificed himself for the whole of mankind, it is in no way a tragic ceremony. On the contrary, we can be glad and thankful, thankful from the bottom of our hearts for everything that he has done for us. For his death was not the end of everything! His death was the *beginning* of everything! After his death he rose again. And because he rose again *we* shall rise again, and so our deaths will not be the end of everything either. This is what we can constantly remember, you and I, through all the things which cause us distress and suffering from day to day in this world; this is what we can constantly and joyfully bear in mind, and constantly be thankful for.

Now you can understand why the Mass, as a memorial ceremony, is at the same time a *thanksgiving* ceremony. The words "think" and "thank" come from the same root. If we think really deeply about any great and splendid thing that has happened to us and for us, then our thinking about it naturally passes into thanks for it. And then we want to express it, to show in words or deeds that we are glad about all that has happened on our account. And so, you see, the great memorial which is the Mass (*thinking* about what happened) is the great *thanks* giving of the whole Church and of each separate congregation, in which we all express our thanks, not only silently and pri-

vately in our own rooms, but all together, for all that
our Lord has done for us in his life, death and resurrection. That is why we pray and sing, praising, thanking,
and offering, and that is why, in thankful remembrance, we eat the body of the Lord under the form of
bread and drink his blood under the form of wine.
That is why the great eucharistic prayer begins with
the solemn summons "Lift up your hearts! . . . Let
us give thanks to God our Lord!" That is why it goes
on "It is in truth fitting and right, just and whole-
some, to give thanks to you, always and everywhere,
holy Lord, almighty Father, eternal God, through
Christ, our Lord." That "through Christ our Lord"
sums everything up that Christ has done for us and for
which we thank the Father through Christ.

Nowadays, as you will have heard, instead of the
word "Mass" (which is actually a rather late Latin
word, difficult to understand: missa-dismissal, depar-
ture), another word, "Eucharist," is often used. This
is a Greek word, used by the early Christians, and
means "thanksgiving."

And now I can answer your question, was it always
like this? The Mass has always been the same ceremony
of remembrance and thanksgiving, the same meal, but
it has by no means always been just as it is today. At

the beginning it was a quite straightforward, simple ceremony, without any extras. Let us take a look backwards, in imagination, to early Christianity—say, the second century. It is the time of repression and persecution! Christians are a dwindling minority. We are looking at a room in Rome, probably a dining-room. Only a short while ago the Eucharist used to be celebrated, as it was by Jesus himself in the upper room, actually during supper. But now, the dining-room has been turned into a meeting-room. All the tables have gone except one, at which the leader of the assembly is standing: the bishop or the priest, in ordinary Roman civil dress, facing towards the people.

They have just brought him some quite ordinary bread and ordinary wine. Now the bishop begins the celebration of Mass. In Greek, using words of his own, he says the *prayer of thanksgiving*, the *eucharistia*. He weaves into this prayer the scriptural account of the last supper. At the end of this prayer of thanksgiving, all those present say "Amen," and receive in their hands, standing, a share of the gifts, which are now no longer simply bread and wine but the body and blood of Christ under the forms of bread and wine.

Such is the Mass as described to us by Justin Martyr

about the year 150: an extremely simple ceremony consisting of one single thanksgiving prayer and the communion of all those present, and hence called "*eucharistia.*" The earliest pattern that has been recorded and handed down to us of the Mass as it was at Rome is that of Hippolytus of Rome and dates from 215. I am sending it to you on a separate sheet; you can see very well from it what the early form of Mass was like. And if you look carefully, you can see which elements in it are still included in our prayer of thanksgiving (the Preface and the Canon) today.

Quite early on, this thanksgiving and meal, which was the whole of the Mass of the early Church, was combined with a liturgy of the word, of reading. It was the same sort of thing as was customary in the Jewish Synagogue. Before the meal there was a reading of a continuous series of texts from the Old and New Testaments.

All this may perhaps make it easier for you to understand the Mass as it is today, which seems so terribly complicated to you. Basically, our modern Mass has a very simple, easily intelligible plan. It consists of the prayer of thanksgiving (with the words of re-presentation, the account of the last supper), and communion. This basic plan was maintained all down the centuries, though developed in many ways, often to the point of being obscured. Essentially, it remains just what the Scriptures tell us of Christ's last supper.

The differences, at the beginning, were these: the whole form of the Mass was very flexible, with only the main lines laid down. Every bishop or priest shaped the liturgy for his own community according to his own ideas and the particular tradition of that community. The language, as I said before, was the spoken language of the time; the oldest Roman liturgy was not in Latin but in the language then spoken in the Roman Empire, Greek. The whole thing was a very intimate, community affair, with everyone joining in the prayers and the singing. And, a very important point: everyone present at the eucharistic meal communicated. A meal without eating, or a communion before Mass or before the prayer of thanksgiving was finished (things that used to be done in our part of the Church not long ago), would have seemed completely nonsensical to the early Christians. And it would have been unthinkable to have several Masses going on at the same time: if there were several priests present, they would all celebrate one single sacrifice together.

Was it always like this?

But that's enough for now. This letter has been longer than I intended. It will have to last you for some time, won't it?

Description of a Mass of the year 215 by Hippoly-tus of Rome (this text is still in use in the Church of Ethiopia):

Straight after the consecration of the bishop, the gifts are brought to him. Together with the priests who are present, he stretches his hands over them, and begins: "The Lord be with you." The answer is given: "And with your spirit."—"Lift up your hearts!"— "We have them with the Lord."—"Let us give thanks to the Lord."—"It is fitting and right!"

Then the bishop continues: "We thank you, O God, through your beloved servant Jesus Christ, whom in the last times you have sent us as saviour and deliverer and messenger of your decree. He is your inseparable Word, by him you made all things, and they were pleasing to you. You sent him from heaven into the womb of the Virgin; borne in the womb, he became flesh, and he was revealed as your Son, born of the

Holy Ghost and the Virgin. In fulfillment of your will, obtaining for you a holy people, he stretched out his hands in suffering, to redeem from suffering those who believe in him. And being handed over of his own free will to suffering, in order to cancel the power of death, to break the bonds of the Devil, to tread under foot the world below, to enlighten the just, to set up a landmark and to proclaim the Resurrection, he took bread, and giving thanks to you he said: Take and eat, this is my body, which is broken for you. *So too the cup, saying:* This is my blood, which is shed for you. When you do this, do it in memory of me. *Mindful then of his death and Resurrection, we offer you the bread and the cup, while we* thank *you that you have regarded us as worthy to stand before you and to serve you. And we pray to you to send the Holy Ghost upon this offering of the holy Church. While you gather her together in unity, may you grant to all the saints, who here receive, the fullness of the Holy Spirit, for the strengthening of the faith in truth, so that we may praise you and honor you through your servant Jesus Christ, through whom is glory and honor to you, the Father, and to the Son with the Holy Ghost, in your holy Church, now and for all eternity. Amen."*

FIFTH LETTER

Our liturgy

You're certainly hard to satisfy! If I tried to answer all the questions in your last letter, I'd find myself writing a book! And just before the beginning of term, too! Some of it will have to be put off to the next time we meet (when?). For the moment, it may be best if I begin at the beginning of your questions. I wrote to you before about Mass in a second-century house. What you ask is, how did that Mass turn into the Mass of the present day? I'll describe as well as I can, in a rather simplified way and in a few sentences, how it got to this point.

The age of persecution is over. Christianity is dominant in the Roman Empire. We no longer need to go to a private house in Rome if we want to join in a Mass of this period—say, of the fifth or sixth century. We can go to one of the magnificent Roman assembly-hall churches, called basilicas. Here stands the wooden table which used to stand in a private house. The bishop or priest still celebrates the same liturgy of commemoration and thanksgiving as before, the same Mass. The priest still stands at the table facing the people, in ordinary civil dress. But a great deal has changed.

Everything is on a larger scale, longer and more ceremonious. Prayers of petition have been inserted in the old, simple prayer of thanksgiving: petitions for the living, for the dead, for various needs, for the Church, etc.; and these prayers include the names of martyrs, to whom, with the persecution period just over, more and more honor is being paid. Outside the prayer of thanksgiving, the singing of psalms has been introduced at three particular points: a psalm with a prayer at the beginning, for the entrance of the clergy into the basilica (the entrance chant or Introit), a second psalm when the faithful bring up the bread and wine and other gifts (the Offertory), and a third psalm at the communion of the faithful.

At this period, too, a whole series of ceremonies had been taken over from the ceremonial of the Roman (especially the East Roman) Imperial Court, including some which earlier Christians had rejected as pagan: genuflections, bows, kisses, and things like incense and lights and special marks of distinction like the stole, the ring, and various other things. Musically developed singing by specially trained singers was tending to replace the singing of the whole congregation. From about the year 250, the liturgy was no longer celebrated in Greek but in Latin: since, even in Rome, the people no longer spoke Greek but had returned to Latin, this adaptation had been made.

You will realize now that a great deal of what, as you tell me, strikes you as strange and unintelligible in the Mass as it is today dates not from Christ or the apostles but from the period which I have just been describing. You need to be understanding about this. As a matter of fact, the Church has already begun to simplify ceremonies again (for instance in the new Holy Week liturgy) and to give things a more straightforward form.

But history went still further. The center of gravity of world history shifted towards the north. As early as the eighth and ninth centuries, political leadership had moved over to France. At the same time, the form of liturgy which had till then been used only in and around Rome and in the Anglo-Saxon missions was transplanted into France. This had far-reaching consequences.

Until now there had been no such thing as a silent

Mass: all the prayers, including the words of consecration, were spoken out loud; this was the way that Christ himself and the apostles had done it. But now numerous *silent* prayers were added in, especially at the beginning (the prayers at the foot of the altar), during the preparation of the gifts, and at the communion. The priest at the altar is now required to keep up an unbroken stream of prayer, even during the actions that he performs. And even the ancient prayers, even the prayer of thanksgiving itself (the Canon), with the words of institution, begin with the passing of time to be said silently. Not the least important factor which makes this possible is the fact that the people no longer understand Latin. So it doesn't matter whether the prayers are said aloud or silently.

The separation between the altar and the people becomes, alas, more and more emphasized. In earlier times the Christians simply stood round the table with the gifts and understood every word of the prayers and readings. Now the language of the liturgy has become unintelligible. Genuflections, signs of the cross and incensings are multiplied more and more. Finally the choir, for the clergy, is cut off from the nave, for the people. The altar-table, which used to stand, well in sight, near the people, becomes the "high altar," which, in time, gets pushed right back against the far wall of the church. Generally speaking, the priest no longer celebrates Mass facing the people, but facing the wall; the altar is so built up that he wouldn't be able to see over it anyway. Because people no longer understand the words of the Mass, it begins to be explained visually. It is thought of as a great spectacle, a drama of the life of Jesus. There is all too little remembrance that this service of thanksgiving is also a meal, to be eaten and drunk. Little remains for the people to do except just watch. It is at this time that the vestments, kept on since late Roman times, begin to be part of the spectacle, with definite, varying colors. In the thirteenth century the practice was begun (though it was forbidden) of lifting up the sacred species during the words of institution, showing them to the people, and worshipping them by kneeling. To receive communion had, alas, become exceptional. So people wanted at least to *see* the body and blood of the Lord. Earlier, communion at Mass had been normal; now it had become the great exception, a form of special "devotion." Earlier, the bread of life had, as Jesus required, been eaten; now, since the High Middle Ages, what was done with it first and foremost was to gaze at it and adore it (this was when the monstrance was introduced). Instead of ordinary bread, it becomes more and more the rule to use an unleavened, snow-white "host," hardly like bread at all. And whereas in the early Church all the priests would celebrate one and the same Mass together, now each priest celebrates his own Mass. This is why more and more side altars are built in the churches along with the main altar. Thus several Masses are celebrated at the same time on different altars.

We must not disguise the fact that in the late Middle Ages a great many abuses, and in many cases monstrous excrescences, had got into the Mass. This is one reason why the Reformers set themselves against the Mass. In the Catholic Church, too, people had realized that it was urgently necessary to reform the Mass. The reforming Council of Trent eliminated a great many of these abuses. And so that such abuses could never come again in the future, the exact form of the Mass was laid down in every particular, which had never been the case before. Everything, down to the smallest detail, was made the subject of an official ruling (even the position of the priest's fingers, and every single word he said). No opportunity was opened up for the people to take any active part. More and more "devotions" came into existence, which the people liked better. More candles were lit at them than at Mass. You could understand the prayers and readings at the devotions; you could join in the praying and singing yourself. None of this was possible at Mass. Only too often, in consequence, Mass was regarded as just one more devotion amongst others (if perhaps the most important), whereas the Mass was instituted by Christ himself, and devotions only by men.

In these circumstances it will certainly not surprise you that quietly, all over Europe, there took place a withdrawal from the Mass. In one country after another it was realized, with dismay, that often only a small fraction of the faithful was still going to Sunday Mass. This naturally, as you can imagine, had a bad effect on the people's religious life. Certainly it was not *only* the strange and unintelligible form that Mass had taken which was to blame for the fact that people were no longer coming in such numbers to the liturgy. But it certainly was *partly* to blame. Hence it is not surprising that our Church's leaders took steps to counteract it. Pius X began in 1900, when he called for active participation in the liturgy by the faithful, and for frequent communion. Later

Popes have followed him, especially Pius XII and John XXIII. The fasting regulations, which used to be so strict, have been greatly relaxed. Evening Masses have been introduced, the rubrics have been simplified, and the vernacular is used at least in the administration of the sacraments. The liturgy of Easter Night, which in later centuries used no longer to be celebrated at night, was restored to its place, and the whole liturgy of Holy Week has been renewed.

Thus our Church stands today in the very midst of a renewal of the liturgy, a renewal of divine worship. You realize that yourself. No doubt we are nowhere near the end of it. The renewal is going on. But let us be glad that so much has been achieved already. Even if we still do not understand everything that is said and read at the altar, we can at least, when we have a community Mass, join in the prayers and singing as the early Christians did, we can join aloud in praising and thanking, and receive the body of the Lord under the form of bread. You, I am sure, will gladly join in. You see, it isn't simply a matter of externals. Liturgical rearrangement on its own isn't enough. It's a matter of doing everything from one's heart. All that counts is simply a better and better, more faithful, more meaningful carrying out of the will of Christ, who said "Do this in commemoration of me."

Good-bye for now. If you want to pursue these questions still further, I'll give you something to read on the subject.

N.B. You can get further information from the works of J. A. Jungmann, e.g.:

On the prayer of thanksgiving: *The Eucharistic Prayer* (Notre Dame, Ind.: Fides, 1958), 55 pages.

On the history of the Mass: *Public Worship* (London, 1957), 249 pages.

If you want something really solid and scholarly, I can lend you *The Mass of the Roman Rite, Its Origins and Development (Missarum Sollemnia)* (New York: Benziger, 1951), two volumes and 958 pages; but there is a one-volume edition of 552 pages.

Today, the rigidity is beginning to give way. Forms that seemed turned to stone are coming to life again. The Church is feeling that she no longer needs the protection of rigidity. Just as under Pius XI in the Lateran Treaty the Church surrendered the external protection of being a secular power, which had seemed necessary in the rough Middle Ages, so now, under Pius XII, she has begun to cast off the protective armor which has till now enclosed the hallowed forms of the liturgy. Pastoral needs are beginning to have, as of old, a deciding voice: those pastoral needs which gave birth to the forms of the liturgy in the early days of the Church.

What an astonishment it was to many of the faithful in our day when they were suddenly able to follow, with understanding, the great course of the liturgy on Easter Night; when they suddenly realized: "This liturgy is ours."

Our liturgy

The mists are beginning to clear. Bright daylight is streaming in. The Church is gathering herself together in new strength. She is going boldly forward to meet the coming ages, as the worshipping People of God.

—JOSEF ANDREAS JUNGMANN
at the Liturgical Congress at Assisi, 1956.

Christians—divided for ever?

Is it going to go on till the Last Day, you ask, this terrible division in Christendom? How long are we going to have friends and sweethearts, colleagues, workmates, even quite often the father and mother of one family going to different churches? How long is every parish going to go on needing two pastors and two churches? How long do marriages and families and pastoral work and the whole Christian people have to go on suffering from this division in faith?

You are right to get impatient. We have been patient far too long, much too patient. We had grown accustomed to the schism. Catholics and Protestants had fought wars against each other. They, who were brothers in Christ, had taken arms against each other and brought endless bloodshed and suffering upon mankind—and said that it was "for religion." When they grew tired of weapons, they called a halt to their hot war; but they only changed it into a cold one:

they fought with pen and ink, with books and newspapers, with violent words and loveless deeds, treating fellow-Christians as though they were men without God. Or, what was almost worse, they didn't even fight any more: they had become so estranged from each other that they hardly even saw each other. They scarcely knew each other any longer, except from the outside, and that only from the worst angle. Mutual prejudice, ignorance, misunderstanding, distrust, suspicion, stand-offishness, arrogance and total absence of penitence (in both) poisoned the atmosphere between the Christian confessions.

But you know, too, that a great deal has altered in these last years. The two World Wars have not been without effect on the Christian confessions, nor have the persecutions that both have had to endure together from the Brown and Red dictatorships. It was easier to rediscover each other in concrete shelters and cellars, in prisons and concentration camps, than in universities and common rooms: many things that had seemed important before became unimportant then. We became aware once more of our common faith. We became aware once more of everything that Catholics and Protestants have in common: the same God and Father, the same Lord Jesus Christ, the same bap-

78

tism, the same word of God in the Scriptures, the same Lord's Prayer. . . .

But the reunion of separated Christians is still a very long way away. Shall we live to see it? And yet it is just *today* that it is so vital for us to come together again, *that the world may believe!* How is the world going to be able to believe us Christians when we try to bear witness in the Church of Christ, if we keep contradicting each other? Who is going to believe two brothers who state contradictory things? Who is going to believe two missionaries who claim to be preaching the same Christ, but preach against each other? Who is going to believe two pastors who both claim to be winning men for Christ, but who work against each other? Do you know the extent to which Catholics have increased in proportion to the whole population of the world in the last eighty years? I just happened to see the statistics recently. And I was deeply shocked to see what a minute amount of progress we have made. Between 1880 and 1958 the proportion of Catholics in the world population rose by only 0.14%!

So that the world may believe, so that our testimony to Christ may be a good and true testimony, we Christians must become *one*. If we are not one, the

79

world will not believe. This is the very reason why Christ prayed for it in the hour of his passion: "Not for them only [the disciples] do I pray, but for them also who through their word shall believe in me: that they *all may be one,* as thou, Father, in me, and I in thee: that they also may be one in us: *that the world may believe that thou hast sent me*" (John xvii. 20-21).

Now you see why we long for reunion: not, for instance, out of fear of Communism, or of the materialism that we have here in the West. But because our Lord himself willed it and prayed for it, just so that the world might believe! Only 28% of the human race are Christians. And of these only half are Catholics, the rest being Protestant, Orthodox, or of various sects. But *how* can all these various Christian confessions come together in one great unity? There are good ways and mistaken ways.

You yourself must surely know Catholics who think that the way to do it is for us to call all other Christians back into our Church. We merely have to admonish them, saying, "Look, we are the one, holy, catholic and apostolic Church; in us you will find everything that you need; it's high time you came back!" This is how these Catholics talk, as though there were nothing for *us* to do. As though we, like the elder brother in the gospel, could stop arrogantly and self-righteously at home when our Father himself has gone out to meet our brother and bring him home. It's no use demanding that the others come back unless we go out to *meet* them! We have been calling to the Orthodox in vain for nine hundred years, and to the Protestants for four hundred. We can't sit about in proud idleness, as though our Church did not bear a share, and a large share, of the guilt of schism, as though our Church did not have a duty, and a grave duty, to clear away obstacles and energetically prepare the way.

There are other Catholics who think that reunion can be attained by the conversion of *individuals*. Conversion certainly can be the solution in a personal crisis of faith. And it is certainly true that the Catholic Church has gained great riches from converts who did not, when within our Church, simply condemn their own past, but made it fruitful. But individual conversions have not brought about the reunion of separated Christian confessions as whole communities. Four hundred years of schism in north-western Europe and nine hundred of schism from the East have shown only too clearly that reunion cannot be reached by individual conversions. All too often our Catholic statistics have only counted those who are converted to us. All too often we have failed to count those who have left the Catholic Church. All too often we have forgotten to count the people who have abandoned any connection with any religious communion and become completely tepid and indifferent. In 1956, for instance, in Western Germany, 16,500 people came into the Catholic Church, and 6,500 came back who had formerly been Catholics. But the records of that same year showed 30,000 people as leaving the Church. Individual conversions alone will not bring about the reunion of separated Christian confessions.

You yourself suggest what's wanted: what's wanted is that we should be better Catholics. As Pope John XXIII has said, ". . . by busying ourselves with every-thing which most needs, on the Catholic side, to be healed and strengthened, according to the teaching of our Lord." This is the true road to reunion. And, no question about it, a hard road; to quote the Pope, a "laborious task." It's not a matter of simply keeping God's ten commandments better. Obviously we have to keep striving to do that too. But what we have here is a quite special task, a task which is in a quite special way directed towards the *others*.

How can reunion be reached? How can we get to

the point where the others will no longer hold apart from us? By carrying out their justified desires, fulfilling their justified demands. The Orthodox, the Lutherans, the Anglicans, the Free Churches, did not separate themselves from us out of mere ill-will, but because (allowing for the very many different factors which play their part in a schism) they considered that there were certain good and necessary things for which there was no room, no understanding and no freedom in the Catholic Church. The Reformers wanted, for instance, to have a liturgy which would be once more a genuine, intelligible service of thanksgiving for everything that Christ has done for us; not a Mass whispered by the priest all by himself in a foreign language with the faithful hardly knowing (until translated missals were brought in only a few decades ago) what was being read or what prayers were being recited; but a Eucharist (thanksgiving) of the whole priestly people of God, with everybody joining aloud and with understanding in the thanks and the prayers and the singing and the eating and drinking. If you compare the silent low Mass of a few years ago (or even an unintelligible Latin High Mass) with the community Mass as we normally have it today, you'll see how many of the justified desires of the Protestants have been fulfilled amongst us in the meanwhile. We can expect further progress in this direction before long.

You see, when faced with the protest of Protestants protesting against the Catholic Church, it's up to us—so far as there is a right element in the protest—to make it unnecessary. This applies to other good demands made by Protestants, too: the importance of the Scriptures to the Church and to the individual believer, for which nothing else can be a substitute; the position of the laity in the Church as the people of God, with a share of responsibility; freedom in the Church from all forms of unjustified ecclesiastical pressure; and not just a veneer of adaptation to individual countries but the real thing, with a reduction of the Latinism of the Church both in missionary countries and those of European culture, etc.

You will realize by now that we don't have to give up hope for reunion. If we keep firmly moving along the road to meet them, then the others, as time goes on, cannot fail to come towards us in the same way, by boldly carrying out on their side the justified desires and expectations that *Catholics* have. If Catholics and Protestants both look into the mirror of the Gospel, and both keep measuring up more and more to the demands of our Lord in the Gospel, then we shall, step by step, come nearer to each other. Then we shall not have to postpone the reunion of separated Christians to the Last Day. But you will also realize that all this is not just a matter of negotiations by Church leaders and discussions by theologians; it's a matter of every individual, including you in your situation, joining in and helping to renew the Catholic Church in preparation for the reunion of separated Christians.

P.S.   In answer to your question about my last letter: no, I'm afraid I can't satisfy your curiosity. I don't know what the "Mass of the Future" will look like. But here's something that I recently read in the paper:

"It is not possible to make precise predictions. But the reforms already made by Rome (especially in the liturgy of Holy Week), the expressed desires of the international liturgical congresses, and the researches of the theologians all point in one definite direction. The decisive factors will be: an increased resemblance to the one determining model given by Christ and the apostolic Church and thus at the same time a greater concentration on essentials and a more intelligible rite. In the concrete, this would mean: (1) For the liturgical *meal*, saying the Eucharistic Prayer, with the words of institution, aloud and intelligibly (i.e., a simplification of the Canon and Preface as they are at present, on the model of the Eucharistic Prayer of Hippolytus, by eliminating the mementos, etc.; with, instead, prayers of petition during the preparation of the gifts); (2) for the litury of the *word*, meaningful congregational prayer and singing and audible, intelligible proclamation of the sacred text, with at least a brief explanation (paying attention to the *whole* of Scripture, e.g. by changing to a four-year cycle for the Sunday readings and having continuous serial reading, at least of the New Testament, on weekdays). Both involve the use of the vernacular, Mass facing the people, more active participation by the people, differentiation between the simple and solemn forms of Mass, and new forms for solemn feast (combined with congregational choral singing, use of wind and string instruments; and a renewal of the singing of the psalms) and the suppression of things of secondary importance (combining together feasts of saints, eliminating unnecessary doubling of prayers, having fewer bows, genuflections, kisses, and incensings, cutting out the last Gospel—which are all in line with the reforms already introduced for Holy Week and Lent). When these reforms will come, it is impossible to say. We have seen in recent years that things often go faster than was expected." This was in the Lucerne paper *Vaterland* on April 1st, 1961.

Many *Churches in this sense imply many* Lords, *many* Spirits, *many* Gods. *There is no question about it: to the degree to which Christendom exists in Churches which are really different and opposed to each other, to that degree she is denying in practice what she acknowledges in theory, the unity and uniqueness of God, Jesus Christ, the Holy Ghost.*

Whatever good reasons there may be for the beginning of such schisms, whatever serious obstacles there may be to ending them, whatever interpretations and extenuations may be made of them, nothing alters the fact that every schism is as such a dark riddle, a scandal.

And in regard to this scandal, the whole of Christendom ought at least to be one in this, that we can think of it only as a constant subject of repentance, *and not, on any of our parts, a repentance to be expected from others, but one in which we are willing to go to meet the others, cost what it may.*

Anyone who is prepared to come to terms with schism in the Church, anyone capable of being at ease with it, anyone to whom the sight of the obvious faults and errors in the other side, and hence their responsibility for it, provides a reason for being tranquil about it, may be a good, loyal believer in some sense that belongs to his particular denomination—a good Roman or Calvinist or Orthodox or Baptist—but he must not think that he can possibly be a good Christian.

—Karl Barth.

Outside the Church no salvation?

Dɪᴅɴ'ᴛ ʏᴏᴜ really know what to say to your Protestant friend's funny story? Two Protestants got to heaven. They wandered all over it and found that everything was perfectly lovely. But one day they came to a high wall. They walked along it, and along and along till they came back to their starting point, completely puzzled. So they applied to St. Peter: "What's the point of that long high wall?" To which St. Peter replied, "That wall's got the Catholics behind it: we mustn't let them know that there's anyone else in heaven besides them."

You're right, of course, that it isn't enough to answer a story like that simply by saying no. That won't do. After all, we say ourselves that the Catholic Church is "the one ark of salvation for all," that outside the Church there is no salvation. And it would be difficult to deny that at least in some countries there are Catholics, even today, who think that, apart from a certain number of exceptions, people of other faiths just don't get to heaven. They are very ready to quote such texts as "He that is not with me is against me: and he that gathereth not with me, scattereth."

Did you know that the reverse is in the Scripture as well? Not only "He that is not with me is against me" but also "He that is not against us is for us." Isn't this a contradiction? Doesn't there have to be a radical decision, an either-or, for Christ or against Christ, belief or unbelief? Yes, this is indeed *the* decision of human life: there is no middle way between belief and unbelief. There is no neutral ground between Christ and Antichrist where you can sit comfortably down and rest and avoid the fighting. This is where we apply the harsh text, "He that is not with me is against me."

Can the opposite be true at the same time, you will ask: "He that is not against us is for us"? Well, what do you do when two passages of Scripture seem to contradict each other? You look in the Bible itself and see how exactly each text fits in: what the context is in which it occurs, and how, consequently, the text that seems obscure is to be understood. Do you know the context of "He that is not against us is for us"? Unfortunately, it is one of the many passages of Scripture that is never read and explained to us on Sundays.

At that time John said to Jesus: "Master, we saw

one casting out devils in thy name, who followeth not us: and we forbade him, because he followeth not with us." But Jesus said: "Do not forbid him. For there is no man that doth a miracle in my name and can soon speak ill of me. *For he that is not against us, is for us.* For whosoever shall give you to drink a cup of water in my name, because you belong to Christ: Amen, I say to you, he shall not lose his reward." (Mark ix, 37-40.)

Do you realize what has been happening here? Here is a man who is not on the side of the Evil One, not against Christ. Nor is he neutral; he isn't hesitating, undecided between Christ and the evil spirits. He knows where he stands; he is on Christ's side. He *believes* in him, he comes out in favor of him, he fights for him against the evil spirits. Indeed, he uses Christ's name, and in that victorious name he casts out the evil spirits.

But, and this is the great *but* that John has against him, "he followeth not with us." He doesn't join in. He has not become one of the group of disciples to which John belongs. He goes out against the evil spirits separately from them. He has the same goal as the disciples, but he goes his own way. He has not joined the Church which is just coming into existence. He is for

Christ, he works for Christ, but he doesn't take any part in his Church.

Why not? We are told nothing about that. All that we know is that this man has nothing against Christ, he believes in him and works for him. But he has something against the group of disciples. So his not joining in has nothing to do with Christ; it has something to do with the disciples. And the unknown man still doesn't toe the line when John remonstrates with him and tells him that he's only allowed to cast out devils if he joins the band of disciples. He doesn't join even when told by John that if he doesn't join he isn't to cast out devils! He takes no notice. He goes right on casting out devils in the name of Jesus.

It's not surprising to find John hurrying to Jesus to tell him the whole story! It's perfectly clear to him that this won't do. The Master himself will have to intervene, straighten things out and put a stop to the activities of this man who is exercising authority outside the band of disciples. John is quite convinced that Jesus is on his side and that he, John, is about to be commended and the stranger put in the wrong.

Far from it. Jesus' answer comes like cold water on John's red-hot zeal: "Do not forbid him!" So John is to stop doing the very thing that he thought he was doing for Christ. He is not to be bigoted and fanatical and arrogant. He is not to make out that good is bad, and forbid it and try to prevent it, merely because it is being done *outside the band of disciples.*

Doesn't John realize that he is being a Pharisee? That he is making himself out to be better than that other man? Whereas he has no reason at all to imagine himself as anything on account of being chosen by Christ; whereas he and all the disciples are poor, sinful human beings; whereas he and the other disciples are possibly the very reason why the stranger doesn't want at any price to join the band of disciples: they, with their arrogance and their false sense of mission and their ambition and their fanatical zeal. So the stranger says to himself: "No, I shouldn't feel at home in a group like that, I can't join in with them. I'll work for Christ, but not with his disciples. I'll work for Christ *outside* the group of disciples."

And Christ said, "Do not forbid him." He understands this stranger. He does not criticize him, or condemn him, or attack him. On the contrary, he explicitly acknowledges the good that is being done through him. And it is his will that this good shall not be obstructed, but go on being done. It certainly isn't at all that he advises John to take the same course. He certainly doesn't want John to separate himself from the band of disciples and go his own way too. Perhaps, indeed, he hopes that the stranger will find his way into the community in the end. But however that may be, Jesus sees and recognizes what is good even outside the community of disciples.

Indeed, Jesus goes a great deal further. He says: This stranger, even though he does go his separate way, really belongs already in a hidden and mysterious way to the community; he already believes and has good intentions and good will. Even though the disciples, in their false zeal and narrowness, won't see it, even though the stranger himself in his obstinacy won't realize it, it's still true: he already belongs to the community of disciples, he is already (though it does not show externally) a member, he already belongs to the Church, is already within the Lord's grace. There is endless depth and all-embracing mercy in Jesus' words: "He that is not against us is for us."

And so someone who does good for Christ's sake, someone who does not belong outwardly to the community of disciples but is an invisible member of it, is also included in the great promise which is made to all true believers, wherever they may be: "Amen, I say to you, he shall not lose his reward."

Now do you understand why I went so far afield to answer your question? It's true that the case of that stranger is not precisely the same as that of a Protestant Christian. But the main thing is the same: We understand our Catholic Church as being the ancient Christian community, standing in the special, official apostolic succession. Protestants do not join in with us, and it is often, alas, we in the Catholic Church (like the disciples then), with our many inadequacies, who are partly to blame for the fact that these others do not want to join in. We can assume, as Jesus did, that Protestants are not on the side of evil, that they are not *against* Christ. Nor are they neutral, standing undecided between Christ and the evil spirits. They are on Christ's side, they are *for* Christ. They believe in him and work for him, doing good for his sake to their neighbor. So Jesus' words, "Do not forbid them," apply to them too. Let them go on doing good, even though they do not join in with you. Don't be conceited and arrogant, loveless and proud towards them. This certainly does not mean: separate yourself from the Catholic Church and become a Protestant. But it does mean: believe that Protestants who sincerely believe in Christ and work for him with the best of intentions already belong to Christ along with us: "He that is not against us is for us." And that consequently they, like us, will find salvation and their heavenly home: "He shall not lose his reward."

Now do you see what is meant by "outside the Church no salvation"? Not some hard, pharisaical truth, but a truth that is deeply merciful, reaching out to all men of good will. What it asserts is that there are not two or several true Churches in which Christ is given to us, but only one: one great all-embracing one. Only those are excluded from her who do not believe because they are against Christ, not by ignorance but by malice; for these unbelievers there is no salvation. All men of good will believe in her, who truly believe in Christ and work for him in love. True, there are different ways of believing, different ways of belonging to the Church. It's true that a Protestant Christian, who rejects the Petrine office which was willed by Christ, does not belong to the Church in the same way as a Catholic does. But the Protestant Christian does belong, if he is in good faith, to the same one Church, the one ark of salvation for all. God does not let anyone be lost except through their own fault; he let his Son die for *all* men, and wills that *all* men should be saved. But whoever is saved is saved through Christ in the Church, and thus belongs in some way (often a very hidden way) to the one Church. Thus the Church is here for all men who are in good faith and of good will. Thus she is the one Church for the salvation of all true believers, outside which there is no salvation but only damnation and unbelief.

Now do you see why that joke misses the point? There are no walls in heaven. We can both be glad about that.

We must hold fast to the truth
that no one is guilty
in the Lord's eyes
of this sin of not belonging to the Church
if he lives in invincible ignorance
of the true religion.
But who would presume to think
that he could determine the cases
in which it is no longer possible
for such ignorance to exist,
when all these cases are different
according to the differences of nations
and of countries
and of the circumstances of individuals.
                                    —PIUS IX.

EIGHTH LETTER

What happens to pagans?

I WAS AMUSED by your answer. Yes, there is something in your idea that *all* the Christians in heaven, even and especially Protestants, are behind the great wall. For they *all*, and many Protestants in particular, think in principle that only Christians can get to heaven.

Well, it probably isn't generally put as bluntly as that. But you are right in thinking that many Christians today, if faced with the question "What happens to pagans?" are simply nonplussed. Earlier, people were very much of the opinion that those who were not baptized were automatically excluded from heaven. Many missionaries, like St. Francis Xavier, accepted all the appalling dangers of missionary work in those days because they were convinced that those whom they didn't baptize would be damned. Ideas became milder as time went on. People said, "We don't know what their fate may be. Scripture does not tell us." But I realize that this, of course, is not a satisfactory answer either.

But only recently, you tell me, this problem has become really vivid for you, because for the first time in your life you have had the opportunity of talking to an Indian boy; it is, of course, getting more and more usual to meet pagans in Europe in this way. This boy you met had no desire to know anything about faith in Christ. It struck you that the conversion of pagans in this modern age is in some ways even more difficult than it was of old. Not because there is any lack of good will in them, but because the difficulties seem insuperable. You didn't have anything like enough time to enter into any real discussion of Christ and belief in him. But you did have the distinct impression, "This young man isn't any worse that I am." Indeed, many things that he told you, quite calmly and modestly, about himself showed that in many respects he was better than you. No wonder you no longer felt inclined to say "Because you are not baptized, you can't go to heaven." Or "Our God hasn't given me anything encouraging to say about your fate." You say that an answer of this sort would have struck you as arrogant and pharisaical. Just because you had the good fortune to be a Christian, you would get to heaven; and just because he, without any fault of his own, had the misfortune not to be a Christian, he wouldn't get to heaven, or at any rate we have received nothing encouraging from God that we can say about his fate.

Now I don't need to tell you that it isn't enough to be baptized in order to get to heaven. Neither a baptismal certificate nor payment of church dues nor even going to Mass on Sundays is any guarantee that you will go to heaven. A Christian, and a Catholic Christian, can be damned too. But what you are asking is "Can a non-Christian be saved?"

It is very hard to answer this question in a letter. It certainly has not always been seen with the same clarity, and this is because people were not always in a position, as they are today, to take account of how enormously numerous non-Christian humanity is. If you ask why, I can give three reasons.

The first is that non-Christian history has been hugely prolonged backwards. You realize what I mean: Christ came a round two thousand years ago. Indications given in the Old Testament which were for a long time regarded as historical (which they are not) made it possible to work out 4145 years before Christ. But modern scientific research estimates the age of humanity at perhaps 600,000 years. In comparison with those 600,000 years, the whole of Christian history (and of the history of the Chosen People of Israel) is an insignificantly small fraction. Were all the people in the remaining round 590,000 years damned? And if not, how are they supposed to have been saved?

The second reason is that the non-Christian world has been enormously increased in terms of space. You know that knowledge about the inhabited globe was extremely limited in ancient times. It's true that people did travel (you will have heard of the great campaign of Alexander the Great as far as India). But taking it as a whole, for the men of the early and mediaeval Church the "world" (or the "inhabited earth" = *oikoumene*) was the Mediterranean area with its hinterlands and neighboring territories. It was only the discoveries of modern times that showed how huge the inhabited earth was, what a huge number of human beings there were in parts of the world that had hitherto been unknown: North and South America, the whole continent of Africa, the wide steppes of Asiatic Russia, the huge plains of India and China, the islands of the Pacific—lands which had, in many cases, very old and advanced cultures, in which the determining force was religion. Countless millions had lived here for thousands of years, before anyone had preached faith in Christ to them. And even today, nearly five hundred years after the discovery of America, in many of these countries only a tiny fragment is Christian. Take for example only these Asian countries with hundreds of millions of inhabitants:

In India only 2.6% of the population are Christians (1.4% Catholics).

In China only 0.66% are Christians (0.5% Catholics).

In Japan only 0.49% are Christians (0.23% Catholics).

The total population of the world today is said to be more than 2500 million. Of these only 847 million are Christians, and of these only 460 million are Catholics.

But what you must notice particularly is that in a relatively short time this low proportion of Christians will get even lower, for the non-Christian peoples of Asia and Africa are increasing at a furious rate in comparison with the Christian peoples of the western world. The latest calculations give the following figures for China:

China in 1960: 700 million (more than the whole of Europe and the Soviet Union).

China in 2000: 1700 million (a good 400 million

more than there are today in Europe, the Soviet Union, North and South America and Africa combined).

All this makes the question more urgent than ever; the number of non-Christians is growing on an enormous scale and at enormous speed. Are all these millions of people damned? And if not, how are they supposed to be saved?

The third reason is that the non-Christian world has thrust its way deep into the Christian world. In the Middle Ages there was such a thing as a "Christian West." Paganism was outside, round the edge of the Christian world. Today paganism—neo-paganism as people call it—is in the midst of the Christian West. The Church is more and more becoming a minority. How many people there are today even in Christian countries who know nothing of Christ, who do not believe in him, who perhaps do not even believe in God! How many there are who are only nominally Christians: Christians by baptismal certificate, but to whom the Gospel of Christ means nothing! And how many superstitions there still are within the true faith!

Here too we must see things as they are. It's true that things are rather better, according to the evidence, amongst Catholics than amongst Protestants; but in

Germany only about 47% go to church on Sundays, in Austria only 33%. It has been estimated that with very few exceptions there is no major town in the western world (including North and South America) in which more than 30% of the Catholics are practising. In places where the Christian tradition no longer carries any weight, the percentage is still lower: in the working-class and industrial districts of Vienna it is 10%, in Paris 6%, in Lens (in the coal-mining area of northern France) 2.66%. Things are no better in Italy: only about 15-16% of those baptized consider themselves bound to go to Sunday Mass; and the picture is even more depressing when this figure is broken down: only 5-7% of young people come, only 2-3% of men.

Who would dare to maintain that all those who don't come are evil men of ill-will? How can they help, in very many cases, having no Christian faith? Suppose they are let down by their parents, or the Christian school, or the parish? Think of all the influences there are from their social milieu, from political parties, and so forth. There's no counting the number of pagans through no fault of their own in Christian Europe. And are all these countless millions of neo-pagans now living within the "Christian world" damned? And if not, how are they supposed to be saved?

If you put together everything that I've said so far, you will see what a painfully acute problem it is: compared with the total population of all the continents of the world throughout the past 600,000 years of human history down to the present day, truly believing Christians are only an insignificantly small minority. Hence the question: what happens to the thousands of millions of others? Can they be saved or not?

Now it should be possible for all thinking Christians to be agreed about two fundamental things. First of all, no one can be saved by his own strength, through his own efforts; he is sheerly dependent upon God's saving grace, which works through Jesus Christ. But, secondly, God does not will anyone to be lost without fault of his own; he wills that everyone should be able, through Christ, to reach his salvation: "God will have all men to be saved, and to come to the knowledge of the truth. For there is one God: and one mediator of God and men, the man Christ Jesus, who gave himself a redemption for all" (I Tim. ii. 4-6); ". . . we hope in the living God, who is the Saviour of all men, especially of the faithful" (I Tim. iv. 10).

From this you can work out two things. In the first place, it is wrong to say: "All religions are equal. They merely express the truth in different ways. Everyone can be saved in his own way. Just do right and don't let anyone scare you." We Christians, on the contrary, believe that no one can be saved through Buddha or Mohammed or any of the prophets, but only through the grace of God in Jesus Christ.

But it is also wrong to say: "Only Christians can be saved. There is no truth except in Christianity. There is no grace except inside the Church." As against this, we Christians believe that *all* men, wherever and whenever they have lived, can be saved by the grace of God in Jesus Christ.

But how is this possible? In the Middle Ages, when the number of the pagans was supposed to be extremely small, it was thought that God would send an angel or a shipwrecked missionary to such men (thought of as being on some lonely island in the middle of the sea), or give them a special illumination at the hour of death, so as to preach the faith of Christ to them. But such solutions are contrary to all experience. It is not possible to suppose that extraordinary, miraculous means are applied to countless millions of people, so as to become in practice the rule, the normal way of salvation.

But what if we suppose, seeing that it is God's merciful will that *all* men shall be saved, that Christ's grace reaches right out beyond the visible Church to embrace the whole of mankind? Even the early Christians were convinced that the grace of Christ had been effective for the pagans *before* Christ, who could not know Christ, and that it was able to bring them to salvation. But really, the majority of mankind is still, today, *before* Christ: they have not heard of him, or not in the right way. Christ has not yet been preached to them. And yet Christ's grace embraces them and can bring them to salvation.

St. Paul the apostle was of all people most deeply convinced that every man stands before God as a sinner and that no one can be saved without God's grace and mercy, which has to be received in a state of faith. This applies equally to Jews and pagans. But just because Paul is so convinced of this, he firmly rejects the idea that the Jews, to whom it was given to have the special revelation of God ("the Law"), should pass judgment on the pagans and think that only they, the Jews, could attain salvation. It is not a question, Paul says, of hearing the "Law," but of doing it.

It is God's grace alone that justifies sinful man. But he who is justified by God's grace has to prove his faith by works of love. God will judge this at the Last Judgment: "Not the hearers of the law are just before God; but the doers of the law shall be justified" (Rom. ii. 13). For in the Judgment, God will "render to every man according to his works. To them indeed, who, according to patience in good work, seek glory and honor and incorruption, eternal life: but to them that are contentious, and who obey not the truth, but give credit to iniquity, wrath and indignation" (Rom. ii. 6-8). It is not impossible for the pagan thus to do good by God's grace: "Glory and honor and peace to every one that worketh good, to the Jew first and also to the Greek [i.e. pagan]" (ii. 9).

But how can the pagan, who does not know the Law, the revelation of God, fulfill the Law? Has he a law, then? Yes, says Paul, God's law is written in the hearts of the pagans, so that they are a law to themselves: "When the Gentiles, who have not the law, do by nature those things that are of the law; these [Gentiles], having not the law, are a law to themselves" (ii. 14). Thus it appears that God has written a law in the hearts of the pagans and that the pagans' conscience gives testimony of God's law: "They show the work of the law written in their hearts, their conscience bearing witness to them, and their thoughts between themselves accusing, or also defending one another" (ii. 15). But in the end God will judge the pagans too according to the Gospel of Christ, as Paul has proclaimed it: "In the day when God shall judge the secrets of men by Jesus Christ, according to my gospel" (ii. 16).

All this, as you see, is not easy to understand. It can be misunderstood. As though it were simply a matter of men's doing good works. This is what the Pharisees thought. No: no man, pagan or not, can do anything good of himself. He is, right from the start, absolutely dependent on God's grace. In the Cross and Resurrection of Christ God has shown himself gracious towards all men, adjudging them righteous. A man has to abandon himself to God empty-handed, without works, putting his whole trust in him; in short, he has to believe. It is only from this state that he can then fruitfully do the works of love. And only thus can he finally face the Judgment.

But all this, this justification of the sinner and his selfless, trusting abandonment to God, can happen in the case of pagans: in a hidden obscure way, not perceptible to us, and not such that we can affirm it with certainty. If a pagan surrenders himself in faith, in some obscure but real way, to the one true God in Jesus Christ, of whom he is perhaps only dimly aware under a hundred concealing veils, and if he then shows forth this faith in works of love, then he can be saved. How this happens, and whether it happens in any particular case, we cannot know. It is God alone who knows all these ways; it is he alone who must judge the individual.

We can be glad that God's grace, as it is revealed to us in Christ, is so vast and wide that it embraces the whole world: all men are within his good pleasure. We can be glad that we do not need to condemn any of these pagans in Asia or Africa or in the middle of Europe. As witnesses to the faith and apostles of Jesus Christ we may and should proclaim the Gospel to them, in the knowledge that God's grace in Jesus Christ has already reached out to embrace them. It is true that none of them can count upon this for himself: for how should he have any certainty about it? If it ever becomes a real decision for him, it is rather a question, for him, of really learning to know that Christ in whom he is already saved.

All this was rather hard going for you, wasn't it? If you haven't understood this letter, read it over quietly again later on. Perhaps you will also read for yourself St. Paul's Epistle to the Romans or the Acts of the Apostles, where you will also find something on this subject.

PRAYERS OF THE PAGANS*

FORSAKEN AM I

Alone, forsaken am I,
By the senses am I tormented,
Alas, distressed like a worm
When the ants crawl over him!
But Thou, Thou wilt not forsake me? . . .

Me, who cannot help but be afraid
If I am separated from Thee,
Like a fish that jerks and struggles
In the dried-up river bed,
O do not Thou forsake me!
—MĀNIKKAVĀSHAGAR, *Southern India, 9th century.*

*Quoted from *Opfer des Wortes, Gebete der Heiden aus fünf Jahrtausenden.* Ed. Paul-Werner Scheele (Paderborn, 1960).

TO LOVE WITHOUT SELF

Lord, I desire no wealth, no children and no learning.
If it is Thy will, I will go on from rebirth to rebirth;
only keep this one thing safe for me, that I may love
Thee without hope of reward, loving without self
for love's sake.

—VEDA, *India, about a thousand years B.C.*

I AM A STRANGER

O *my Lord,*
If I pray to Thee from fear of hell,
Then banish me to hell!
If I pray to Thee from hope of paradise,
Then shut me out from it!
But if I pray to Thee for Thine own sake,
Then do not withhold from me anything of Thine
  eternal beauty!
O *my God, I cannot live in the world without*
  remembrance of Thee,
And how could I endure the world to come
Without the sight of Thee?
O *my Lord, my sighing is nothing before Thee;*

What happens to pagans?

*For I am a stranger in Thy land, alone
In the midst of them who honor Thee.*
　　　—RABIA AL-ADAWĪYA, *Mesopotamia, c. 717-801.*

GIVE LIGHT TO MY FACE

*My God, who bringest the clear light of day
Over the land, to me is day so dark,
Nothing for me but grief, distress and pain!
Sorrow and suffering have overwhelmed me,
As one whose only portion is all tears. . . .
O Thou my God, O Thou who art my Father,
Thou who begot me, to my face give light!
How long must I continue thus forsaken,
How long lack thy protection over me?*
　　　　　　—SUMERIAN LAMENT,
　　　　　　Southern Babylonia, c. 1700 B.C.

COME TO ME, O GOD

*Come to me, O God
And care for me.
It is Thou alone who dost anything for me;*

121

Other than Thee no one does anything for me,
Thou art the only one.

Come to me, O God, returning day by day.
Thou art a glorious God.
My heart yearns towards Thy City.
My heart leaps up with joy, my breast is full of
    gladness,
For my prayers and implorings by day
And my songs of praise by night
Have been heard.
My prayers shall pour forth again from my mouth,
And this very day they will be heard.

Thou art the only God, O Sun God,
There is none who is like to Thee.
Thou dost protect millions, Thou dost save hundreds
    of thousands,
Thou art the Protector of all
Who call upon Thee, O Lord of Heliopolis.

Punish me not because of my many sins.
I am a man who does not know himself.

What happens to pagans?

I am a fool.
All the day long I follow the pull of my mouth
Like an ox that follows the grass of the pasture;
But when evening comes, then comes Thy grace,
Like to a coolness pouring over me.

—EGYPT, *2nd millennium B.C.*

NINTH LETTER

Are you superstitious?

PERHAPS YOU LAUGHED like everyone else at the uproar caused all over India a little while ago by the conjunction of the planets Jupiter, Saturn, Mars, Venus and Mercury in the sign of Capricorn. The astrologers had foretold some huge catastrophe—an earthquake, or even the end of the world. Many women went and camped in the open with their children shortly before the critical time began. During both the affected nights Delhi rang with the prayers of Hindu priests keeping up a continual chorus of blessings, at the instance of the inhabitants, directed by loudspeaker over this or that area of the town. Costly gifts were made to the temples. Trains, planes and buses found themselves with very few passengers. No animals were slaughtered, so there was no meat to be had. Prices rose for other kinds of food, because a great many wholesalers closed down for the three days. Masses of employees in public services and private firms took the time off. Even Nehru, making speeches in ridicule of the whole astrological scare, was only able to calm the people to a very limited degree.

Yes, I dare say you laughed, like everyone else, at the superstitious Indians: a thing like that wouldn't happen here! You think not? What's our position with regard to astrology? Haven't you ever, by any chance, managed to find out, just casually, which Sign of the Zodiac you were born under? Whether you're a Leo subject or an Aries subject, or Sagittarius, or Virgo? Wouldn't you by any chance be able to say just what special opportunities *your* star-type would have: what, e.g., you can expect of a person born under Taurus, considering the special abilities, strengths and weaknesses of his type? Many people who smile at the mention of astrology are more or less regular consultors of horoscopes: they just wonder whether it'll come true or not, whether this or that expectation will be fulfilled—good luck, bad luck in an examination, in business, in money, in love? And perhaps, after all, *this* week . . . ? After all, you don't *know*; it can't do any harm.

And so you hear people say that astrology, you know, was not born yesterday. Which of the sciences has so long a tradition as astrology? And how many great astronomers, investigating the natural *law* (nomos) that operates in the stars have at the same time been astrologers, hoping to discover a secret spiritual *meaning* (logos) hidden in the stars? In fact, the earliest astronomers in the history of our culture, the Babylonians, were at the same time great astrologers. Their astronomical theory and practice had important results in the history of science. But those ancient sages were not willing to limit themselves to this. The "art" of Babylonian astrology went beyond this: it consisted in reading the picture language of the stars; it gave names to the stars and interpreted them with reference to earthly events. Thus in very early times the Babylonians, or Chaldaeans as they were later called, built up an astrological language, by means of which they declared and interpreted prophecies from the sky. In the words of a Babylonian text, the seven planets—the sun, moon, Mars, Mercury, Jupiter, Venus, Saturn, by which we still name the seven days of the week—"spin the threads of fate as they pass across the sky; silently they weave the pattern of earthly life." The fame of the Babylonian or Chaldaean astrologers was so great that "Chaldaean" became a professional name for an interpreter of the stars, an astrologer. The Magi of the Gospel, the "wise men from the East" who came seeking the new-born

King of the Jews, were not kings but in all probability Babylonian, Chaldaean, astrologers.

It must be admitted that not even Christianity succeeded in eradicating astrology, which had taken root amongst the Egyptians and Greeks. Christian antiquity and the Middle Ages are both full of star-interpretation. Emperors such as Frederick II and Rudolph II, poets such as Dante and Calderón, Popes such as Julius II and Leo X all went in for interpreting the stars. But what may surprise you more is that even modern scientific astronomy with all its revolutionary discoveries has not been able to root out astrology. The classic names of early modern science were themselves astrologers, at least in their early years: John Regiomontanus, Tycho Brahe, Galileo, Kepler, Francis Bacon and others. Modern astronomers, it is true, are no longer astrologers. But have you never noticed that the same illustrated papers that show pictures on their first or second page of the latest space rocket shot from Cape Canaveral print the week's horoscope on the back page? And you may have heard, too, how having a Mercedes Star on the radiator, the sign of top-level technological progress, doesn't prevent quite a number of drivers from doing certain items of business in accordance with astrological charts!

Indeed, one may ask oneself, what's the use of scientific arguments against the bogey of astrology? The fact that the old cosmos of the astrologers is a fable; that the sacred seven planets of astrology have been increased by the discovery of Uranus, Neptune and Pluto; that between Mars and Jupiter there may be more than two thousand miniature planets; that the Zodiac as used by astrologers no longer coincides with the positions of the constellations; that the stars of Taurus, the Bull, for instance, which can quite easily, with a bit of imagination, be linked up on a piece of paper so as to suggest the bull's horns, are in actual fact on nothing like the same plane as each other, but some of them billions of miles further off in space from our earth than others?

What's the use of telling a believer in astrology that the moment of conception is much more important for a new human being than the moment of birth, that the moment of birth can be advanced or retarded for medical reasons, thus arbitrarily turning a Pisces subject into an Aries subject; that the same time and place of birth will produce both a saint and a criminal, while, on the other hand, people with completely different horoscopes will all be drowned together in one shipwreck? What's the use of saying to a believer in astrology that many people simply read their own traits of character into their Zodiacal type, that the great characteristic of astrological forecasts is to be hopelessly vague and ambiguous, and that, finally, the whole of astrology is a sound money-spinner for astrologers and the press?

You see, all these objections are true. And they've been repeated over and over again. But they don't succeed in killing belief in the stars. For stronger than all these arguments is man's urge to know. To know what his future is, to know what he has to expect. Because man wants to know what he has to expect, and because this is not written anywhere upon earth, he tries to read it in the sky. This is why he supposes that heaven and earth, the stars and man, are all ruled by the same laws, that man is somehow bound by mysterious threads to archetypes in the sky. This is why he tries to discover this mysterious bond between man and his star-image. This is why he seeks to unravel the knot, to interpret the riddle of human destiny. Man longs to know what he has to expect. He longs to be sure. He longs to have control over his destiny and his future.

There is no form of predicting and controlling the future too daft and stupid for modern people to try:

from tea leaves, cards, palmistry, and magic pendulums to primitive dream-interpretation and raising the dead in séances. According to the demoscopic institute at Allensbach, one German in every ten is seriously influenced by some form of soothsaying. And did you know that for many people Friday is an "unlucky day," that people have to have some sort of stuffed "lucky animal" in their car to guard against accidents, that fear of the number 13 is so widespread that many hotels do not have any room numbered 13, as otherwise that room is often left unoccupied? Only recently a man told me how he had been able to occupy a luxury cabin 13 on an ocean liner at a reduced price, because some woman was afraid of the number. And I was told by an engineer recently that he turned back and went home one morning when on his way to the office, because a black cat had crossed his path. That does surprise you, doesn't it: a man of the technological age, as superstitious as that! But you know it often happens that the more faith decreases the more superstition grows.

That the world may believe we ourselves must be firmly *believers*. Superstition poisons faith. But the wretched part of it is that very often particularly devout people mix and deform their faith with gross superstition. It's true that it's not so bad as it once was, when consecrated hosts, relics, holy water, etc., were used for the most horrible superstitious practices. But even today there are pious people who think that they can bring pressure to bear on God with some *particular number* of Masses, or prayer-formulas, or candles: "It's only if there are just so many, and you do it in just this order, and there isn't any break in it, that it works." All this goes on in spite of the fact that the Council of Trent exhorted the bishops "to remove absolutely out of the Church all special numbers of particular Masses and candles, which are rather an invention of a superstitious cult than a true honoring of God." It is not by the performance of any particular formula or custom invented by men that we can look for our prayers to be heard, but from the free goodness and mercy of our Lord. Christians also practice superstition with images of saints, medals, relics and so forth, if they attribute any effectiveness to these mere things as such, instead of to an interior cleaving to God in faith, hope and love. All the sensation-hungry scrambling after miracles, visions, apparitions and private revelations, too, is a superstitious deflection from the center of our faith. Through any superstitious practice, we make our faith unbelievable to the world; we provoke unbelievers and those who believe differently from us to laugh at our Church and our faith.

You see, all superstition about the stars has been ruled out once for all by belief in the one unique great Star! This is the meaning of the Scripture story of the wise astrologers from the East. In Jesus, the Lord, all expectations are fulfilled: the expectation of the prophets and the just men of Israel *and* the expectations of heathen astrologers. You see what I am trying to say: this is what can make you and me so endlessly happy, and what no astrologer or horoscope can tell us: In this *One*, in Jesus, *every* expectation, *all* expectations are fulfilled: the expectations of the whole world. It is not written in the stars, our future is not hidden in the constellations. For us who believe our future is all light and gladness in him who says of himself: "I, Jesus, am . . . the bright and morning star!" (Apoc. xxii. 16).

O the depth of the riches
of the wisdom
and of the knowledge of God!
How incomprehensible are his judgments,
and how unsearchable his ways!
For who hath known the mind of the Lord?
Or who hath been his counsellor?
Or who hath first given to him,
and recompense shall be made him?
For of him, and by him, and in him, are all things:
to him be glory for ever. Amen.

—Epistle to the Romans xi. 33-36.

TENTH LETTER

Do you have doubts?

No, IT DOESN'T show. You give the impression of being very self-assured, of having thought things out very thoroughly. No, it doesn't show at all. But all the same this doesn't surprise me, you know. Or to put it more clearly, I should be astonished if it were otherwise. If it were otherwise, it would be a sign that you were still a child. Of course there are people who remain children in this sense all their lives, but there are not so many of them nowadays. Nowadays, there are innumerable people of your age who are in the same state as you are: outward certainty, inward—doubt. Often piercing and tormenting doubts. They go away again sometimes for weeks at a time, or get covered up by work or the various distractions that make up a human life. But you know very well that they haven't gone away for good, they haven't surrendered, they have merely, for the moment, retreated.

You tell me in your letter that you have often accused yourself of these doubts in the confessional. I don't know whether this was the right thing to do. There certainly are many prayerbooks where you will find the admonitory question "Have you doubted the faith?" But this question is easy to misunderstand and has already caused distress to far more people than was necessary. There is all the difference in the world between doubting the faith because, deep down, one doesn't seriously *want* to believe; because the practical consequences of the faith are uncomfortable, and so one would rather cling to the question and the doubt; and so, instead of bravely and believingly saying Yes despite all the obstacles in the way, one takes refuge behind the obstacles like a slacker and a coward and labels everything with a lazy-minded question mark: "After all, who knows whether any of that stuff is really true?" Between that and, on the other hand, seriously wanting to believe and not shrinking from the consequences of the faith but, with the best will in the world, still having temptations to disbelief; because one is now a thinking Christian at last, not asleep but awake, and aware of the difficulties in the faith; because one feels thoroughly shaken by them sometimes, possibly even violently mixed up and turned upside down. Doubts of this second kind are really better called difficulties. We don't create them for ourselves, they happen to us. But a thousand such difficulties coming as temptations do not constitute one sinful doubt of which one would need to accuse oneself before God.

It doesn't seem to me to be one of the worst features of our age that it forces us to make a decision. In earlier times faith was something obvious for the majority of Christians. One was as it were born into the faith. Just as one was born a Frenchman or Italian, a Hungarian, Spaniard or Swiss, so one was "born" a believer. All quite obvious. "One" believed. Everybody believed: one's father and mother, the whole family, the neighbors, the whole village, the whole town—everyone believed. True, even then it wasn't quite as sure as all that; even then there were a certain number of unbelievers and numerous frivolous, lazy-minded doubters. But at least it seemed outwardly as though everyone believed—so, after all, why not I?

But all that is over nowadays. You tell me yourself what a shock it was to you, during these last years, as you began to see a bit more deeply into real life. You got to know other people, at school, at work, at parties. They were often extremely likable, but the faith wasn't something obvious to them. They had other beliefs or—so they said—believed nothing at all. You read about highly intelligent men who taught quite different ideas from those of your parents and your priest. Of course they hadn't lied to you; but suppose they had been mistaken? And how many parents are there who don't believe themselves? It's not surprising that you began to wonder.

But, to repeat, it isn't a bad thing for you to have been pushed into deciding. Faith isn't something that you can simply get by inheritance, like any other characteristic of body or soul. Even baptism is no use unless it is matched with the decision of faith; baptism is the sacrament of faith. Faith means decision: are you going to rely ultimately on yourself or on God? Are you going to take everything self-sufficiently into your own hands or leave everything selflessly to him? Are you going to trust his word or not, believe or not believe?

It's quite clear that a child could not be faced with this decision in the same way that you are. A child takes a great deal for granted which you can't take for granted any more, and don't need to. Your knowledge in every field has increased. Your idea of the world has changed and broadened. You are living in a different environment. All this is not irrelevant to your faith. Your faith is going through a crisis of growth. It's still the same, but what it wants is to become the faith of an adult. Anyone who thinks he can go through the whole of life with nothing but the catechism is trying, as an adult, to climb mountains in his baby shoes.

But you ask, What am I to do when I get into these crises of faith? Keep calm and don't worry! The great Russian writer Leo Tolstoy has said: "If the thought comes to you that everything that you have thought about God is mistaken and that there is no God, do not be dismayed. It happens to many people. But do not think that the source of your unbelief is that there is no God. If you no longer believe in the God in whom you believed before, this comes from the fact that there was something wrong with your belief, and you must strive to grasp better that which you call God. When a savage ceases to believe in his wooden God, this does not mean that there is no God, but only that the true God is not of wood." So what is needed is to think things over quite calmly and unworriedly. During these years you will certainly have to be stripping off many things which are mere superficial coverings of the faith. When something comes loose in your religious ideas, this does not by any means always mean that something has come loose in the faith. You told me yourself once how your uncle, even though he has read about it, always thinks, when there are changes in the liturgy, that something in the faith itself has been changed, and that he is strangely unable to understand how the Mass, always the same, can have changed so much during the centuries. And it was just the same with yourself over something similar: as a child you thought that the world had been created by God literally in six days, meaning six times twenty-four hours. I can remember your telling me later on that the six days were six million years. In the end you realized that this wouldn't do either: how could light have been created on the first day when such bodies as the sun, moon and stars were only created on the fourth? How were you to fit in the whole order of things in the biblical account of creation with the findings of modern astronomy and geology? Now you know that the six days are simply the poetic dress in which the writer has clothed his faith in God the Creator. Now you know that these are all images and figures in which to express that everything, every single creature, was made by God by his free choice, and that to him alone adoration is due. Now you know that the Scripture doesn't aim at teaching science and that everywhere in Scripture—including the accounts of the creation of man and the Fall—you have to distinguish between the dogmatic content and the form of presentation. Thus you are learning to understand the word of God better and better. Scripture, it has been said, is like the sea: the further in you go, the deeper it gets.

You see, what at first appears as a difficulty, an obstacle to faith, can if rightly understood lead to a deepening and strengthening of the faith: it means that one does not stop short at external and superficial things but presses on into the depths; one does not content onself with the letter of Scripture but seeks in everything for the spirit. Thus your faith changes and yet still remains the same. You become more mature. I don't need to tell you that this doesn't always happen automatically. Everyone has to depend on his neighbor's help. When you have difficulties with your faith, you can often be helped by a sermon or a book or a lecture or (after all, you can't always be writing to me) a talk with a priest or some friend.

But, you know, nothing that I have ever written to you provides any sort of final answer. Questions of faith are not like riddles or crossword puzzles: with things of this sort it may take one some time to find the solution, but once it's found, everything is clear and simple. It is completely different with the faith. Here we have, not human truth which men can state and understand, but God's truth, which goes far beyond any statement or understanding of man's. The faith never becomes clear. The faith remains obscure. Not until we enter into glory will it be otherwise: "We see now through a glass in a dark manner: but then face to face. Now I know in part: but then I shall know even as I am known" (I Cor. xiii. 12). Only when we are in glory will it be otherwise. Until then there will always be more difficulties coming up, more doubts coming up: there are *bound* to be. Doubt is the shadow cast by faith. One does not always notice it, but it is always there, though concealed. At any moment it may come into action. There is no mystery of the faith which is immune to doubt.

But from this you will realize, too, the greatness and audacity of faith. Faith is an adventure; an adventure as daring as climbing along a knife-edge thirteen thousand feet up. Of course one is liable to feel scared when one sees the empty space on each side. Of course one is liable to wonder whether one is ever going to manage to get past it. But what is the right thing to do? Not to keep looking down into space and lose your balance, but to keep bravely and firmly on; not to rush it, but go quietly and steadily step by step, keeping your eyes on the next key point.

When doubt gets hold of you, the thing to do is to trust in God, and not to leave go of Christ and his grace, not to lose hold on him. In moments like that, even when you cannot see any solution, you mustn't weaken. You must carry your faith through the difficulty, believing here and now and in spite of it! There is one thing you can always do in a crisis: pray for faith. There is nothing automatic in the fact that you believe. Your belief is a gift of the Holy Ghost. It isn't a gift that you have once for all. You need to keep on praying for it. Even though you do believe, you are constantly threatened by unbelief. And so it is so consoling and encouraging for us to have the prayer of the man in the gospel, who believed but was threatened by unbelief and said: "I believe, Lord: help my unbelief."

And another thing: you are not alone. Christ has not called you to believe all on your own. He does not expect you to fight your doubts alone. He has called you into the Church. The Church is simply the great community of all believers, guided and sustained by the Holy Ghost. So you are not alone, you are in the Church. You are in that great community of believers which, ever since the days of the apostles, has been carrying, sustaining each individual believer so that the faith shall not, in his loneliness, become too heavy a burden for him. That community of believers is carrying you, too. In that community you are sheltered, and united with all those all over the world who believe in Christ. What you believe is not just a private idea of your own. What you believe is the faith of the Church, that faith which goes back to the apostles—no, to the risen Lord himself.

As a member of that great community of believers, oughtn't you to have the strength not only to preserve your faith but to radiate it? In this correspondence we have kept coming back to the subject of the *believableness* of the Church: of how important it is that, amid all the distress of our times, the Church should stand before the world as believable, *that the world may believe*. But, you know, it can't be done by saying, "The Church—oh, yes, the Church ought to be believable so that the world may believe." Who is the Church? Is the Church just something hovering above our heads between heaven and earth? Or is the Church just a sort of bureaucratic machine? Is the Church just the "organization" of the Pope, the bishops and the clergy? No, *we* are the Church, all of us who believe in Jesus

Christ, the great community of believers, of which the Pope and bishops and priests (who have to be believers too) are servants. All of *us* are the Church, you and I. And in the end, when you get right down to it, it doesn't depend on great speeches or large-scale action whether the Church is going to stand before the world as believable, but on you and me. The world consists of an endless series of small, overlapping circles. In the middle of each circle stands a Christian, one individual Christian, standing for the Church. And the one question that matters is whether this Christian is being luminous, whether his faith is radiating light and warmth and love. Whether the world is to believe depends on you!

The day after tomorrow I am going on holiday. You won't be hearing from me for some time. But you will surely have plenty to chew over in all that I have written to you recently.

I WISH TO BE A MAN OF THE CHURCH AND NOT TO BE CALLED AFTER THE FOUNDER OF SOME HERESY BUT BY THE NAME OF CHRIST AND TO BEAR THAT NAME WHICH IS BLESSED UPON EARTH: AND IT IS MY DESIRE TO BE CALLED A CHRISTIAN BOTH IN DEED AND IN SPIRIT

IF I · WHO SEEM TO BE THY RIGHT HAND · WHO BEAR THE NAME OF PRIEST AND HAVE TO PROCLAIM THE WORD OF GOD · OFFEND IN ANY WAY AGAINST THE CHURCH'S TEACHING AND THE RULE OF THE GOSPEL SO THAT I BECOME A SCANDAL AGAINST THEE · THE CHURCH · THEN MAY THE WHOLE CHURCH IN ONE COMMON DECISION · CUT OFF ME · HER RIGHT HAND · AND CAST ME FROM HER

—*Words of Origen, one of the greatest theologians of the early Church.*